Fueling Your Success The Power of Motivation

khalid

Fueling Your Success The Power of Motivation
Copyright © 2023 by khalid

The first edition was published in 2023

ISBN:

Published by:
Sunshine
1663 Liberty Drive
Hyderabad, IN 47403
www.Sunshinepublishers.com

This book is self-published using on-demand printing and publishing, which allows it to be printed and distributed globally

TABLE OF CONTENT

Chapter 1: Understanding Motivation   06

The Importance of Motivation

The Definition of Motivation

Different Types of Motivation

Chapter 2: The Science Behind Motivation   12

The Psychology of Motivation

The Role of Dopamine in Motivation

Understanding Intrinsic and Extrinsic Motivation

Chapter 3: The Benefits of Being Motivated   18

Increased Productivity and Efficiency

Improved Focus and Concentration

Enhanced Goal Achievement

Chapter 4: Discovering Your Motivational Drivers24

Identifying Personal Values and Passions

Setting Meaningful Goals

Recognizing and Overcoming Obstacles

Chapter 1: Understanding Motivation

The Importance of Motivation

In today's fast-paced and competitive world, motivation plays a crucial role in achieving success and personal growth. It is the driving force that propels individuals to overcome obstacles, reach their goals, and unleash their full potential. Whether you are a student, an entrepreneur, an athlete, or a professional, understanding the power of motivation is essential for fueling your success.

Motivation is more than just a desire to achieve something; it is a mindset that keeps you focused, determined, and resilient in the face of challenges. When you are motivated, you have a clear vision of what you want to accomplish, and you take consistent action to make it a reality. It helps you stay committed to your goals, even when the journey becomes tough.

One of the key reasons why motivation is crucial is that it provides you with a sense of purpose. When you have a strong motivation, you have a reason to wake up every morning and work towards your dreams. It gives you a sense of direction and helps you prioritize your time and efforts. Without motivation, you may find yourself drifting through life without a clear purpose, feeling unfulfilled and dissatisfied.

Motivation also boosts your self-confidence and belief in your abilities. When you are motivated, you believe that you can overcome any challenge that comes your way. This self-belief acts as a catalyst for taking risks, stepping out of your comfort zone, and seizing opportunities. It allows you to push past your limitations and achieve things you once thought were impossible.

Furthermore, motivation fuels resilience and perseverance. It helps you bounce back from failures and setbacks, instead of giving up. Motivated individuals see failures as learning opportunities and use them to grow and improve. They understand that setbacks are temporary and keep pushing forward, even when the going gets tough.

Lastly, motivation enhances productivity and efficiency. When you are driven by a strong motivation, you become more focused and disciplined. You prioritize tasks, eliminate distractions, and manage your time effectively. This heightened productivity allows you to accomplish more in less time, giving you a competitive edge in your personal and professional endeavors.

In conclusion, the power of motivation cannot be overstated. It is the foundation of success and personal growth. By understanding its importance and harnessing its power, you can unlock your full potential and achieve extraordinary results in all aspects of your life. So, fuel your success with motivation and watch yourself soar to new heights.

The Definition of Motivation

Motivation is a fundamental concept that drives human behavior and fuels success in all aspects of life. It is the force that propels individuals to take action, set goals, and persevere in the face of challenges. In this subchapter, we will delve into the depths of motivation, exploring its various dimensions and understanding its power to transform lives.

At its core, motivation is the internal drive, desire, or passion that compels individuals to act in a certain way. It is the burning fire within, pushing people to go beyond their comfort zones and strive for greatness. Motivation can be intrinsic, stemming from an individual's own values, interests, or personal fulfillment. Conversely, it can also be extrinsic, driven by external factors such as rewards, recognition, or societal expectations.

The power of motivation lies in its ability to provide individuals with a sense of purpose and direction. It gives them the energy and enthusiasm to pursue their goals, overcome obstacles, and persist in the face of adversity. Motivated individuals are more likely to exhibit higher levels of commitment, resilience, and determination, ultimately leading to greater success in their endeavors.

Understanding the sources of motivation is crucial to harnessing its power effectively. Some people find motivation in the pursuit of personal growth and self-improvement. Others are driven by a desire to make a positive impact on their communities or the world at large. Additionally, external factors such as financial incentives, recognition, or competition can also serve as powerful motivational triggers.

However, it is important to note that motivation is not a one-size-fits-all concept. Each individual is unique in what inspires and drives them. What may be motivating for one person may not hold the same significance for another. Therefore, it is essential to identify and tap into individual motivations to unleash their full potential.

Fueling Your Success: The Power of Motivation explores the multifaceted nature of motivation and provides practical strategies for cultivating and sustaining it. By understanding the definition of motivation and its various dimensions, readers can gain valuable insights into how to harness this powerful force to fuel their own success.

Whether you are an entrepreneur, student, athlete, or professional, motivation is the key to unlocking your full potential. By embracing the power of motivation, you can overcome obstacles, achieve your goals, and create a life filled with purpose and fulfillment. This subchapter serves as a stepping stone on your journey to harnessing the power of motivation and unleashing your true potential.

Different Types of Motivation

Motivation is a powerful driving force that helps us achieve our goals and fulfill our desires. It is the fuel that keeps us going, even when faced with challenges and obstacles. In the book "Fueling Your Success: The Power of Motivation," we delve into the various types of motivation that can inspire and empower individuals from all walks of life.

1. Intrinsic Motivation: This type of motivation comes from within ourselves. It is driven by our internal desires, values, and interests. Intrinsic motivation is often associated with passion and a genuine love for what we do. When we are intrinsically motivated, we derive satisfaction and fulfillment from the task itself, rather than relying on external rewards or recognition.

2. Extrinsic Motivation: Unlike intrinsic motivation, extrinsic motivation stems from external factors such as rewards, praise, or fear of punishment. It is driven by external incentives rather than personal satisfaction. While extrinsic motivation can be effective in achieving short-term goals, it may not be sustainable in the long run. Therefore, it is important to strike a balance between intrinsic and extrinsic motivation.

3. Achievement Motivation: This type of motivation is fueled by the desire to accomplish specific goals and attain success. Individuals with high achievement motivation are often driven by the need for personal growth, continuous improvement, and a sense of accomplishment. They thrive on challenges and are willing to put in the necessary effort to overcome obstacles and reach their goals.

4. Social Motivation: Social motivation is derived from the need for connection, belonging, and approval from others. It is driven by the desire to be accepted, recognized, and respected within our social circles. This type of motivation can be a powerful

force, as the fear of disappointing others or the need for social validation can push individuals to strive for excellence.

5. Fear Motivation: Fear can be a powerful motivator, although it is often seen as a negative type of motivation. Fear motivation is driven by the desire to avoid negative consequences or outcomes. While fear can provide a temporary boost in motivation, relying solely on fear as a driving force may lead to stress, anxiety, and burnout.

Understanding the different types of motivation can help individuals harness their inner drive and propel themselves towards success. By recognizing which type of motivation resonates with us the most, we can leverage it to set meaningful goals, overcome challenges, and stay focused on our path to success.

In "Fueling Your Success: The Power of Motivation," we explore how to tap into these different types of motivation and use them to our advantage. By cultivating a deep understanding of our own motivations, we can unlock our true potential and create a life filled with purpose, passion, and achievement. Whether you are a student, professional, or entrepreneur, this book will provide you with valuable insights and practical strategies to fuel your success through the power of motivation.

Chapter 2: The Science Behind Motivation

The Psychology of Motivation

Motivation is a powerful force that drives individuals to take action, overcome obstacles, and achieve their goals. It is the fuel that propels success and enables individuals to reach their full potential. Understanding the psychology behind motivation is vital for anyone seeking to harness its power and unlock their own success.

Motivation can be defined as the internal and external factors that stimulate desire and energy in individuals to be consistently engaged and committed to achieving a goal. It is a complex concept that is influenced by various psychological factors. One of the key aspects of motivation is understanding the different types of motivation.

Intrinsic motivation refers to the internal drive that comes from within an individual. It is the desire to engage in an activity for its own sake, driven by personal satisfaction, enjoyment, or a sense of purpose. In contrast, extrinsic motivation is driven by external rewards or incentives, such as money, praise, or recognition. Both types of motivation play a significant role in fueling success, but intrinsic motivation tends to be more sustainable and fulfilling in the long run.

Another important psychological factor in motivation is the power of beliefs and mindset. Our beliefs about our abilities, potential, and the outcome of our efforts greatly influence our motivation levels. Those with a growth mindset, who believe that their abilities can be developed through hard work and dedication, are more likely to be motivated to take on challenges and persevere through setbacks. On the other hand, those with a fixed mindset, who believe that their abilities are fixed and cannot be changed, are more likely to shy away from challenges and give up easily.

Understanding the psychology of motivation also involves recognizing the role of emotions. Emotions can either fuel or hinder motivation. Positive emotions, such as excitement, enthusiasm, and joy, can boost motivation and increase engagement with a task or goal. On the other hand, negative emotions, such as fear, anxiety, and frustration, can demotivate individuals and lead to avoidance or procrastination. Learning to manage and regulate emotions is crucial for maintaining high levels of motivation.

In conclusion, the psychology of motivation is a fascinating field that explores the internal and external factors that drive individuals to take action and achieve their goals. By understanding the different types of motivation, the power of beliefs and mindset, and the influence of emotions, individuals can harness the power of motivation to fuel their success. Whether you are a student, professional, entrepreneur, or athlete, understanding the psychology of motivation can be a game-changer in achieving your full potential and reaching new heights in your personal and professional life.

The Role of Dopamine in Motivation

In our quest for success, motivation plays a crucial role. It is the driving force that propels us towards our goals, fuels our ambition, and keeps us going even in the face of challenges. But have you ever wondered what exactly happens in our brain that makes us feel motivated? The answer lies in the fascinating neurochemical called dopamine.

Dopamine is a neurotransmitter that acts as a chemical messenger in the brain. It is often referred to as the "feel-good" chemical, as it is associated with pleasure, reward, and motivation. When we achieve something or experience a pleasurable event, dopamine is released, creating a sense of satisfaction and reinforcing the behavior that led to that reward. This is what makes dopamine so crucial in the realm of motivation.

Studies have shown that dopamine levels increase in response to anticipation of a reward. It is this anticipation that drives us to take action, to work towards our goals, and to persevere even in the face of setbacks. Dopamine acts as a catalyst, boosting our motivation and helping us stay focused on the task at hand.

Interestingly, dopamine levels can also be influenced by external factors such as social interactions and environmental cues. Positive reinforcement, encouragement, and even small wins can trigger the release of dopamine, further fueling our motivation. On the other hand, negative experiences or stress can decrease dopamine levels, making it harder to stay motivated.

Understanding the role of dopamine in motivation can help us harness its power to achieve our goals. By creating an environment that fosters positivity, providing ourselves with regular rewards and celebrating small victories, we can boost our dopamine levels and keep our motivation levels high.

However, it is important to note that dopamine alone is not the sole determinant of motivation. It is just one piece of the puzzle. Motivation is a complex interplay of various psychological, social, and environmental factors. Nevertheless, dopamine plays a significant role in this intricate process, serving as a catalyst that propels us forward.

In summary, dopamine is a key player in the realm of motivation. Its release in response to rewards and anticipation of rewards drives us to take action and stay focused on our goals. By understanding how dopamine works and harnessing its power, we can fuel our motivation and propel ourselves towards success.

Understanding Intrinsic and Extrinsic Motivation

Motivation is the driving force behind our actions, behaviors, and achievements. It is what pushes us to reach our goals and fulfill our dreams. In the book "Fueling Your Success: The Power of Motivation," we delve into the concepts of intrinsic and extrinsic motivation, exploring how they impact our lives and drive us towards success.

Intrinsic motivation refers to the internal factors that inspire and propel us forward. It is the inherent desire to engage in an activity for its own sake, fueled by personal satisfaction, enjoyment, or a sense of fulfillment. When we are intrinsically motivated, we find joy in the process itself, not just the end result. For example, a musician who spends hours perfecting their craft because they genuinely love playing an instrument is driven by intrinsic motivation.

On the other hand, extrinsic motivation involves external factors, such as rewards, recognition, or social approval. It is the desire to perform a task to attain an external outcome or avoid punishment. Extrinsic motivation can be seen in scenarios where individuals work solely for a promotion, a bonus, or praise from others. While extrinsic rewards can provide temporary motivation, they often lack the depth and lasting impact of intrinsic motivation.

Understanding the interplay between intrinsic and extrinsic motivation is crucial for harnessing the full power of motivation. While both types can be effective in driving us towards our goals, intrinsic motivation tends to have a more profound and lasting impact on our overall success and well-being.

When we are intrinsically motivated, we are more likely to experience higher levels of creativity, engagement, and perseverance. We are driven to excel in our chosen fields because we genuinely enjoy what we do. Intrinsic motivation also fosters a sense of autonomy, allowing us to take ownership of our actions and decisions.

However, extrinsic motivation should not be discounted entirely. External rewards and recognition can serve as valuable reinforcements, especially in situations where intrinsic motivation may wane. They can provide a temporary boost, helping us stay on track and overcome obstacles.

By nurturing our intrinsic motivation and aligning it with external rewards, we can create a powerful synergy that propels us towards success. This combination allows us to find joy in the process while reaping the benefits of external recognition and validation.

In conclusion, understanding the dynamics of intrinsic and extrinsic motivation is essential for fueling our success. By tapping into our innate passions and finding joy in the journey, we can harness the power of motivation to achieve our goals and lead fulfilling lives.

Chapter 3: The Benefits of Being Motivated

Increased Productivity and Efficiency

In today's fast-paced world, the ability to increase productivity and efficiency is crucial for achieving success in any endeavor. Whether you are an entrepreneur, a student, a professional, or simply someone looking to improve your daily life, understanding the power of motivation can be the key to unlocking your full potential.

Motivation is the driving force behind our actions. It provides the energy and determination needed to overcome challenges and push ourselves to achieve our goals. When properly harnessed, motivation can lead to increased productivity and efficiency in every aspect of our lives.

One of the most significant benefits of motivation is its ability to fuel our focus and concentration. When we are motivated, we are more likely to stay on task and avoid distractions. This heightened focus allows us to complete tasks more quickly and with greater accuracy, ultimately saving us time and effort.

Furthermore, motivation empowers us to set clear goals and take proactive steps towards achieving them. By establishing a clear vision of what we want to accomplish, we can prioritize our tasks and allocate our resources effectively. This strategic approach helps us utilize our time and energy efficiently, increasing our overall productivity.

Another important aspect of motivation is its ability to inspire creativity and innovation. When we are motivated, we are more likely to think outside the box and come up with innovative solutions to problems. This creative thinking can lead to more efficient processes and improved outcomes.

Moreover, motivation plays a crucial role in maintaining a positive mindset and overcoming obstacles. It provides us with the resilience and determination needed to persevere through challenges and setbacks. With a motivated mindset, we can approach difficulties as opportunities for growth, rather than insurmountable roadblocks. This positive outlook enhances our problem-solving skills and allows us to find efficient solutions to complex issues.

In conclusion, understanding the power of motivation is essential for increasing productivity and efficiency in all aspects of our lives. By harnessing the energy and determination that motivation provides, we can fuel our focus, set clear goals, inspire creativity, maintain a positive mindset, and overcome obstacles. Whether you are striving for professional success, academic excellence, or personal fulfillment, cultivating motivation will undoubtedly propel you towards achieving your goals and fueling your success.

Improved Focus and Concentration

In today's fast-paced and ever-distracting world, maintaining focus and concentration can be a constant challenge. Whether you are a student trying to study for exams, an employee aiming to meet deadlines, or an athlete striving for peak performance, the ability to concentrate and stay focused is crucial for success. This subchapter explores the importance of improved focus and concentration and provides valuable strategies to enhance these skills.

The Power of Motivation in Improving Focus and Concentration

Motivation plays a vital role in improving focus and concentration. When we are motivated, we are more likely to direct our attention to the task at hand and sustain that focus for longer periods. The power of motivation lies in its ability to provide a sense of purpose and desire to achieve our goals. By understanding what drives us and harnessing that motivation, we can overcome distractions and enhance our ability to concentrate.

Strategies for Enhancing Focus and Concentration

1. Set Clear Goals: Clearly define your goals and break them down into smaller, manageable tasks. This helps create a sense of purpose and provides a roadmap for your focus and concentration.

2. Create a Distraction-Free Environment: Minimize distractions by finding a quiet place to work or study. Turn off notifications on your phone or computer and create a dedicated space free from interruptions.

3. Practice Mindfulness: Incorporate mindfulness techniques into your daily routine to improve focus and concentration. Mindfulness involves being fully present in the moment and can help train your brain to stay focused on the task at hand.

4. Take Regular Breaks: Allow yourself short breaks to recharge and refresh your mind. Research suggests that taking regular breaks can actually enhance focus and productivity.

5. Exercise Regularly: Physical activity has been shown to improve cognitive function, including focus and concentration. Incorporate regular exercise into your routine to boost your mental performance.

6. Prioritize Sleep: A good night's sleep is essential for optimal cognitive function. Lack of sleep can impair focus and concentration, so make sleep a priority in your daily routine.

By implementing these strategies, you can cultivate improved focus and concentration, leading to greater productivity and success in all areas of your life. Remember, the power of motivation is the key to unlocking your ability to concentrate and achieve your goals.

Enhanced Goal Achievement

In the journey towards success, one of the most critical factors that can propel us forward is the power of motivation. Motivation acts as our driving force, pushing us to set goals and work tirelessly towards achieving them. It ignites a fire within us, giving us the determination, resilience, and focus needed to overcome obstacles and reach new heights. In this subchapter, we will explore the concept of enhanced goal achievement and how the power of motivation can fuel our success.

Setting goals is an integral part of the success process. However, merely setting goals is not enough. We need to enhance our goal achievement by harnessing the power of motivation. Motivation acts as a catalyst, transforming our dreams into tangible realities. When we are motivated, we become more disciplined and dedicated towards our goals. We develop a clear vision of what we want to achieve and are willing to put in the necessary effort to make it happen.

To enhance goal achievement, it is crucial to understand what motivates us on a deeper level. Motivation can stem from various sources, such as personal aspirations, external recognition, or the desire to make a difference in the world. By identifying our core motivators, we can tap into a wellspring of energy and determination that will propel us towards our goals.

Another aspect of enhanced goal achievement is the ability to stay motivated during challenging times. We all face setbacks and obstacles along the way, but it is how we respond to them that determines our success. By cultivating a strong mindset and developing resilience, we can bounce back from failures and use them as stepping stones towards achieving our goals. Motivation acts as a shield against negativity and self-doubt, enabling us to stay focused and determined even when the going gets tough.

Furthermore, enhancing goal achievement involves creating a supportive environment. Surrounding ourselves with like-minded individuals, mentors, or coaches can provide us with the guidance, encouragement, and accountability needed to stay motivated and on track. Additionally, adopting effective strategies such as visualization, affirmations, and goal tracking can further enhance our motivation and increase our chances of success.

In conclusion, enhanced goal achievement is a result of harnessing the power of motivation. By understanding what motivates us, staying resilient during setbacks, and creating a supportive environment, we can fuel our success and turn our dreams into reality. Motivation acts as the driving force behind our actions, providing us with the determination, focus, and resilience needed to achieve our goals. So, let us harness the power of motivation and embark on a journey towards unparalleled success.

Chapter 4: Discovering Your Motivational Drivers

Identifying Personal Values and Passions

In our journey towards success, it is crucial to understand and harness the power of our personal values and passions. These intangible elements play a significant role in shaping our motivations, guiding our actions, and ultimately fueling our success. By aligning our goals with our core values and passions, we can tap into an unparalleled source of motivation and drive that will propel us towards our desired achievements.

Personal values are the principles and beliefs that define who we are as individuals. They serve as our moral compass and provide a framework for making decisions and choosing the right path in life. Identifying our personal values is a deeply introspective process that requires self-reflection and self-awareness. By understanding what truly matters to us, we can align our actions and goals with our values, creating a sense of purpose and meaning in everything we do.

Passions, on the other hand, are those activities, pursuits, or interests that ignite a fire within us. They are the things that make us feel alive, energized, and fulfilled. Discovering our passions requires exploration, experimentation, and a willingness to step outside our comfort zones. When we engage in activities that align with our passions, we tap into a wellspring of motivation and enthusiasm that propels us forward, even in the face of challenges.

When our personal values and passions are in alignment with our goals and aspirations, we unlock the true power of motivation. This alignment creates a sense of authenticity and congruence in our lives, enabling us to overcome obstacles, persevere in the face of adversity, and remain focused on our objectives.

To identify our personal values and passions, we can start by reflecting on our past experiences, strengths, and interests. What activities have brought us the most joy and fulfillment? What principles do we hold dear and strive to uphold in our daily lives? Engaging in self-assessment tools, such as personality tests or values exercises, can also provide valuable insights into our core values and passions.

Once we have identified our values and passions, it is essential to regularly reassess and reaffirm them. As we grow and evolve, our values and passions may shift, and it is crucial to ensure that our goals and actions remain aligned with these changes. Regularly reflecting on our values and passions allows us to stay true to ourselves and make decisions that are in line with our deepest desires and aspirations.

In conclusion, identifying our personal values and passions is a pivotal step in harnessing the power of motivation. By aligning our goals with our core values and engaging in activities that ignite our passions, we tap into an unstoppable force that propels us towards success. So take the time to explore, reflect, and connect with your values and passions, and watch as your motivation skyrockets, fueling your journey to success.

Setting Meaningful Goals

In life, it is essential to have a clear direction and purpose. Setting meaningful goals is the key to unlocking your true potential and fueling your success. Whether you are an entrepreneur, a student, or someone looking to make positive changes in your life, understanding the power of motivation and setting meaningful goals can be a game-changer.

Setting meaningful goals provides you with a sense of purpose and direction. It allows you to define what you want to achieve and gives you a roadmap to follow. Without clear goals, you may find yourself drifting through life without a clear sense of fulfillment. By setting meaningful goals, you create a vision for your future and a path to get there.

The power of motivation plays a crucial role in achieving your goals. Motivation acts as a driving force that keeps you focused and determined, even when faced with challenges. It gives you the energy and enthusiasm to overcome obstacles and push through difficult times. When your goals are meaningful to you, your motivation becomes even stronger, as you have a deep-rooted desire to achieve them.

To set meaningful goals, you must first reflect on your values, passions, and aspirations. What truly matters to you? What are your long-term dreams? By aligning your goals with your core values and passions, you create a meaningful connection that fuels your motivation. Remember, meaningful goals are deeply personal and resonate with your innermost desires.

Once you have identified your meaningful goals, it is crucial to break them down into smaller, manageable steps. This allows you to create a clear action plan and track your progress along the way. Celebrate each milestone you achieve, as it will boost your motivation and keep you moving forward.

Additionally, it is essential to remain flexible and adaptable in your goal-setting journey. Life is unpredictable, and circumstances may change. Be open to adjusting your goals when necessary, while staying true to your overall vision and purpose.

In conclusion, setting meaningful goals is a powerful tool for success and personal growth. It provides you with direction, purpose, and the motivation needed to overcome challenges. By aligning your goals with your values and passions, breaking them down into actionable steps, and remaining adaptable, you can harness the power of motivation and achieve extraordinary results in all areas of your life. Start today, and fuel your success through meaningful goal setting!

Recognizing and Overcoming Obstacles

In our journey towards success, we often encounter obstacles that can deter us from reaching our goals. These obstacles can take various forms, such as self-doubt, fear of failure, lack of resources, or even external circumstances beyond our control. However, it is crucial to remember that obstacles are not barriers that prevent us from achieving our dreams; rather, they are stepping stones that help us grow and become stronger individuals. In this subchapter, we will explore the importance of recognizing and overcoming obstacles, and how they can fuel our motivation to achieve greatness.

The first step in overcoming obstacles is to acknowledge their existence. By accepting that obstacles are a natural part of life, we can shift our perspective and view them as opportunities for growth and self-improvement. Understanding that obstacles are temporary and not insurmountable allows us to approach them with a positive mindset.

One of the most effective ways to overcome obstacles is by developing a strong sense of motivation. Motivation is the driving force that propels us forward, even in the face of adversity. By cultivating a clear vision of what we want to achieve and reminding ourselves of the reasons behind our goals, we can strengthen our motivation and stay focused on the path to success.

Another crucial aspect of overcoming obstacles is adopting a problem-solving mindset. Instead of getting overwhelmed by challenges, we should embrace them as opportunities to find innovative solutions. This requires a willingness to think outside the box, seek alternative routes, and learn from past setbacks. By approaching obstacles with creativity and resilience, we can find new ways to overcome them and continue progressing towards our goals.

It is also important to seek support when facing obstacles. Surrounding ourselves with a network of positive and motivated individuals can provide us with the encouragement, guidance, and perspective we need to overcome challenges. Sharing our struggles with others can offer new insights and help us gain a fresh perspective on our situation.

In conclusion, recognizing and overcoming obstacles is an essential part of our journey towards success. By accepting the presence of obstacles, cultivating motivation, adopting a problem-solving mindset, and seeking support, we can transform obstacles into opportunities for growth and personal development. Remember, the power of motivation lies within us, and with the right mindset, we can overcome any obstacle that comes our way.

Chapter 5: Techniques for Self-Motivation

Developing a Positive Mindset

In the journey towards success, one of the most powerful tools we possess is our mindset. Our thoughts, beliefs, and attitudes shape our actions and ultimately determine the outcomes we achieve. The power of motivation lies in our ability to cultivate a positive mindset that propels us forward, even in the face of challenges and setbacks.

A positive mindset is not about denying the existence of difficult situations or pretending that everything is perfect. It is about choosing to focus on solutions rather than problems, seeing opportunities where others see obstacles, and embracing a growth mindset that believes in our ability to learn and improve.

One of the first steps to developing a positive mindset is to become aware of our thoughts and internal dialogue. Negative self-talk can be a significant barrier to motivation and success. By monitoring our thoughts and consciously replacing negative beliefs with positive affirmations, we can rewire our minds to focus on possibilities instead of limitations.

Another aspect of developing a positive mindset is surrounding ourselves with positivity. This could mean seeking out mentors or role models who inspire us, reading motivational books or articles, or even creating a gratitude journal to remind ourselves of the blessings and achievements we have already experienced. By immersing ourselves in positive influences, we can shift our perspective towards optimism and possibility.

Furthermore, it is essential to set realistic goals and celebrate small victories along the way. A positive mindset recognizes that success is not always about reaching the final destination but also about the progress we make and the lessons we learn in the process. By acknowledging and celebrating our achievements, no matter how small, we can fuel our motivation and reinforce our positive mindset.

Lastly, developing a positive mindset requires perseverance and resilience. There will inevitably be obstacles and setbacks on the path to success, but a positive mindset sees these challenges as opportunities for growth and learning. By reframing failures as valuable lessons and refusing to give up, we can maintain a positive outlook and continue moving forward towards our goals.

In conclusion, developing a positive mindset is a powerful tool in fueling our success. By consciously monitoring our thoughts, surrounding ourselves with positivity, celebrating small victories, and cultivating perseverance, we can unlock the power of motivation within ourselves. With a positive mindset, we can overcome obstacles, embrace challenges, and ultimately achieve our goals.

Utilizing Visualization and Affirmations

Visualization and affirmations are powerful tools that can greatly enhance your motivation and help you achieve success in various areas of your life. By harnessing the power of your mind, you can create a clear picture of what you want to achieve and reinforce positive beliefs that will drive you towards your goals. In this subchapter, we will explore the techniques of visualization and affirmations and discover how they can fuel your success.

Visualization is the process of creating a mental image of your desired outcome. By vividly imagining yourself already achieving your goals, you are programming your mind to believe in your ability to make them a reality. Whether you want to excel in your career, improve your relationships, or enhance your health, visualization can be a powerful tool to manifest your dreams into reality. Take a moment to close your eyes and imagine yourself in that desired state. See yourself confidently speaking in front of a large audience, receiving a promotion, or enjoying a fulfilling relationship. Allow yourself to immerse in the emotions associated with the achievement of your goals. By consistently visualizing your success, you train your mind to focus on the positive aspects and attract the opportunities needed to make it happen.

Affirmations, on the other hand, are positive statements that reinforce empowering beliefs and attitudes. By repeating affirmations daily, you can rewire your subconscious mind and replace negative thoughts with positive ones. Create affirmations that are aligned with your goals and aspirations. For instance, if you want to boost your self-confidence, repeat statements such as "I am confident and capable in every situation" or "I believe in my abilities to achieve greatness."

Write down your affirmations and place them in visible locations, such as on your bathroom mirror or computer screen. By reciting them regularly, you will gradually adopt these positive beliefs as your own, boosting your motivation and fueling your success.

Combining visualization and affirmations can be a powerful technique to overcome obstacles and maintain a positive mindset. When faced with challenges, visualize yourself successfully overcoming them and affirm that you have the skills and resources to conquer any adversity. This mindset shift will enable you to stay motivated, focused, and determined in the pursuit of your goals.

In conclusion, utilizing visualization and affirmations can significantly enhance your motivation and propel you towards success. By harnessing the power of your mind, you can create a clear vision of your desired outcomes and reinforce positive beliefs that align with your goals. Practice visualization techniques and repeat affirmations daily to reprogram your subconscious mind and ignite your motivation. Remember, your thoughts shape your reality, so fuel your success by visualizing and affirming the life you desire.

Practicing Self-Discipline and Time Management

In our fast-paced and demanding world, the ability to practice self-discipline and manage our time effectively is crucial to achieving success in any area of life. Whether you are a student, an entrepreneur, or a professional, mastering these skills can fuel your success and propel you towards your goals. This subchapter will explore the power of motivation in developing self-discipline and time management strategies that can transform your life.

Self-discipline is the foundation upon which all achievements are built. It is the ability to control our impulses, resist distractions, and stay focused on our priorities. By cultivating self-discipline, we gain the power to make conscious choices that align with our long-term goals, rather than succumbing to short-term gratification. This requires developing a growth mindset, setting clear and realistic goals, and creating a supportive environment that fosters discipline. Through practical techniques such as creating routines, breaking tasks into manageable chunks, and embracing accountability, we can strengthen our self-discipline muscles and overcome challenges.

Time management is the art of allocating our limited time resource in the most efficient and effective way possible. It involves prioritizing tasks, setting deadlines, and eliminating time-wasting activities. With proper time management, we can increase productivity, reduce stress, and create more time for activities that truly matter to us. This subchapter will provide practical tips for effective time management, such as creating a schedule, setting boundaries, and utilizing time-blocking techniques. Additionally, we will explore the importance of taking breaks, practicing self-care, and avoiding the trap of multitasking.

The power of motivation lies at the core of self-discipline and time management. When we are driven by a strong sense of purpose and fueled by passion, we are more likely to stay committed to our goals and make the most of our time. This subchapter will delve into the various sources of motivation, such as intrinsic and extrinsic factors, and provide strategies for staying motivated in the face of challenges and setbacks. By harnessing the power of motivation, we can overcome procrastination, maintain focus, and achieve extraordinary results.

In conclusion, practicing self-discipline and time management are essential skills for anyone seeking success. By cultivating self-discipline, managing our time effectively, and harnessing the power of motivation, we can unlock our full potential and accomplish great things. This subchapter will provide you with the tools and insights needed to fuel your success and embark on a journey of personal and professional growth.

Chapter 6: Cultivating Motivation in Others

Motivating Employees and Team Members

Motivation is the driving force behind success in any endeavor. Whether you are a business owner, a team leader, or an individual striving for personal growth, understanding the power of motivation and how to effectively motivate others is crucial. In this subchapter of "Fueling Your Success: The Power of Motivation," we will explore the various strategies and techniques that can be employed to inspire and motivate employees and team members.

One of the most important aspects of motivating others is recognizing that everyone is unique and has different intrinsic motivators. Some individuals may be driven by recognition and rewards, while others may be motivated by a sense of purpose or the opportunity for personal growth. Therefore, it is essential to take the time to understand what motivates each individual and tailor your approach accordingly.

In order to foster motivation, it is essential to create a positive and supportive work environment. This can be achieved by providing regular feedback and constructive criticism, recognizing and celebrating achievements, and promoting a culture of teamwork and collaboration. When team members feel valued and appreciated, they are more likely to be motivated and committed to their work.

Setting clear and achievable goals is another powerful motivator. By establishing specific targets and milestones, employees and team members can see their progress and feel a sense of accomplishment. It is important to regularly revisit these goals and provide the necessary resources and support to help individuals achieve them.

In addition to setting goals, it is crucial to provide opportunities for growth and development. Offering training programs, mentoring, and career advancement opportunities can help employees and team members feel challenged and motivated to continuously improve their skills and knowledge.

Another effective way to motivate individuals is by fostering a sense of purpose and meaning in their work. By connecting their tasks and responsibilities to a larger vision or mission, employees and team members will feel a sense of pride and fulfillment in their contributions. This can be achieved through effective communication and regular reminders of the organization's values and objectives.

Finally, it is important to lead by example. As a leader or manager, your own motivation and enthusiasm will have a direct impact on your team members. By demonstrating passion and commitment, you can inspire and motivate others to give their best effort.

In conclusion, motivation is a powerful tool that can drive success in any organization or individual endeavor. By understanding and leveraging the power of motivation, leaders can inspire and empower their employees and team members to reach new heights of achievement. By creating a positive work environment, setting clear goals, providing growth opportunities, fostering a sense of purpose, and leading by example, you can fuel the success of your team and organization.

Building a Supportive and Inspiring Environment

Creating a supportive and inspiring environment is crucial when it comes to fueling your success. Surrounding yourself with positive influences and a strong support system can greatly impact your motivation levels and propel you towards achieving your goals. In this subchapter, we will explore the power of motivation and how to build an environment that fosters it.

Motivation is the driving force behind success. It is what pushes us to overcome obstacles, stay focused, and maintain a positive mindset. Without motivation, it becomes easy to lose sight of our goals and give up when faced with challenges. By understanding the power of motivation, we can harness its energy to propel ourselves towards success.

One of the key factors in building a supportive and inspiring environment is surrounding yourself with like-minded individuals. Seek out individuals who share similar goals and aspirations. Collaborate with them, share ideas, and learn from each other's experiences. By surrounding yourself with motivated individuals, you will be constantly inspired and challenged to push beyond your limits.

In addition to finding the right people, it is important to create a physical space that supports your goals. Whether it is a home office or a designated workspace, having a dedicated area that is free from distractions will help you stay focused and motivated. Decorate your space with motivational quotes, pictures, or objects that remind you of your goals. This will serve as a constant reminder of what you are working towards.

Another important aspect of building a supportive environment is to cultivate a positive mindset. Practice gratitude and focus on the positive aspects of your journey, even when faced with setbacks. Surround yourself with positive energy by engaging in activities that bring you joy and uplift your spirits. This could be anything from listening to motivational podcasts, reading inspiring books, or engaging in hobbies that fuel your passion.

Remember, building a supportive and inspiring environment is not a one-time task. It requires continuous effort and dedication. Regularly assess your surroundings and make necessary adjustments to ensure that you are surrounded by positivity and motivation. By doing so, you will create an environment that not only fuels your success but also inspires and motivates others around you.

In conclusion, understanding the power of motivation and building a supportive and inspiring environment are essential steps towards achieving success. Surround yourself with like-minded individuals, create a physical space that supports your goals, cultivate a positive mindset, and regularly assess and adjust your surroundings. By doing so, you will unlock your full potential and fuel your success in all aspects of life.

Effective Leadership Strategies

Leadership plays a crucial role in the success of any individual, team, or organization. It is the driving force that motivates and inspires others to achieve their full potential. In this subchapter, we will explore effective leadership strategies that harness the power of motivation to propel individuals and teams towards success.

One of the key leadership strategies is setting a clear vision and goals. A leader must have a compelling vision that inspires and excites others. By communicating this vision effectively, leaders can motivate their team members to work towards a common objective. Additionally, setting achievable goals helps to provide a sense of direction and purpose, enabling individuals to stay focused and motivated.

Another important strategy is leading by example. A leader who leads from the front and demonstrates the behavior they expect from others gains the respect and trust of their team. By embodying the qualities and values they want to instill, leaders motivate others to follow suit. This creates a positive work culture that fosters motivation and encourages everyone to strive for excellence.

Effective communication is also a vital leadership strategy. Leaders must be able to articulate their vision, expectations, and feedback clearly and effectively. By fostering open and transparent communication channels, leaders can eliminate misunderstandings and facilitate a collaborative environment. This enables individuals to feel valued, motivated, and empowered to contribute their best efforts.

In addition, a great leader is a skilled motivator. They understand the importance of recognizing and celebrating the achievements of their team members. By providing regular feedback, acknowledging their efforts, and rewarding their accomplishments, leaders can boost morale and inspire individuals to continue performing at their best. This creates a positive cycle of motivation and drives individuals to exceed their own expectations.

Finally, an effective leader is also a lifelong learner. They constantly seek opportunities for personal and professional growth, and encourage their team members to do the same. By investing in continuous learning and development, leaders can stay ahead of the curve, adapt to changing circumstances, and inspire others to do the same.

In conclusion, effective leadership strategies harness the power of motivation to propel individuals and teams towards success. By setting a clear vision, leading by example, promoting open communication, recognizing achievements, and embracing lifelong learning, leaders can create a motivated and high-performing environment. Whether you aspire to be a leader in your personal or professional life, these strategies will help you unlock your full potential and fuel your success.

Chapter 7: Overcoming Motivational Challenges

Dealing with Procrastination

Procrastination is a common struggle that many individuals face, hindering their progress and preventing them from achieving their goals. In this subchapter, we will explore effective strategies to overcome procrastination and harness the power of motivation.

Procrastination often stems from a lack of motivation or fear of failure. When we procrastinate, we delay taking action on important tasks, choosing short-term comfort over long-term success. However, by understanding the power of motivation, we can break free from the cycle of procrastination and propel ourselves towards success.

The first step in dealing with procrastination is to identify the underlying causes. Reflect on why you are procrastinating – is it due to a lack of interest, fear of failure, or feeling overwhelmed? Recognizing these barriers will help you develop a tailored approach to overcome them.

One effective strategy to combat procrastination is to break down tasks into smaller, manageable steps. When faced with a daunting project, it is easy to feel overwhelmed and put it off. However, by dividing the task into smaller, achievable goals, you can build momentum and gradually work towards completion. Celebrate each milestone to boost your motivation and keep procrastination at bay.

Another powerful technique is to practice time management. Create a schedule or to-do list, prioritizing tasks based on their importance and urgency. By allocating specific time slots for each task, you will have a clear roadmap to follow, reducing the likelihood of procrastination. Additionally, consider using time-blocking techniques, dedicating specific periods solely to focus on important tasks.

Accountability is also crucial when it comes to overcoming procrastination. Share your goals and deadlines with a trusted friend, family member, or mentor who can hold you accountable. Regular check-ins and progress updates will keep you motivated and prevent you from falling into the trap of procrastination.

Finally, cultivate a positive mindset and visualize the end result. Remind yourself of the benefits and rewards that await you upon completion of the task. By focusing on the positive outcomes, you will ignite your motivation and push past procrastination.

In conclusion, procrastination can be a significant obstacle on the path to success. However, by understanding the power of motivation and employing effective strategies, you can overcome this challenge. Break down tasks, manage your time effectively, seek accountability, and cultivate a positive mindset. By implementing these techniques, you will fuel your success and achieve your goals, leaving procrastination behind.

Managing Burnout and Rekindling Motivation

Introduction:
In today's fast-paced and demanding world, it is not uncommon to experience burnout and a loss of motivation. We often find ourselves overwhelmed with responsibilities, deadlines, and the constant pressure to perform at our best. However, it is crucial to recognize the signs of burnout and take proactive steps to manage it. In this subchapter, we will explore effective strategies to overcome burnout and reignite your motivation, enabling you to fuel your success.

Recognizing   Burnout:
Burnout can manifest in various ways, including physical exhaustion, emotional detachment, and a lack of interest or satisfaction in work or personal life. It is important to acknowledge these signs and understand that burnout is a legitimate concern that requires attention.

Prioritizing   Self-Care:
One of the most effective ways to combat burnout is by prioritizing self-care. This includes ensuring you get enough rest, maintaining a healthy diet, engaging in regular exercise, and finding activities that bring you joy and relaxation. Taking care of your physical and mental well-being is essential to recharge your energy levels and regain motivation.

Setting   Boundaries:
Often, burnout occurs due to an imbalance between work and personal life. It is crucial to set clear boundaries and allocate time for activities that bring you happiness outside of work. By establishing boundaries, you can create a healthier work-life balance and prevent burnout from consuming your life.

Finding   Purpose:
Rediscovering your sense of purpose can be a powerful tool in

rekindling motivation. Reflect on your goals and values, and align your work and personal life with them. When you have a clear sense of purpose, your motivation will naturally increase, as you will find meaning and fulfillment in what you do.

Seeking   Support:
Don't be afraid to reach out to others for support. Talk to a trusted friend, colleague, or mentor about your experiences and feelings. They may provide valuable insights, advice, or simply offer a listening ear. Sometimes, sharing your burden can help alleviate burnout and reignite motivation.

Embracing   Change:
Lastly, be open to change. If you find yourself continuously burnt out in your current situation, it may be time to explore new opportunities or make changes in your work environment. Embracing change can revitalize your motivation and help you discover new paths to success.

Conclusion:
Managing burnout and rekindling motivation is an ongoing process. By prioritizing self-care, setting boundaries, finding purpose, seeking support, and embracing change, you can navigate through burnout and reignite your passion. Remember, you have the power to fuel your success by taking proactive steps to manage burnout and keep your motivation alive.

Coping with Setbacks and Failure

Failure and setbacks are an inevitable part of life. No matter how motivated or determined we are, there will always be obstacles and challenges that can hinder our progress. However, it is how we cope with these setbacks that truly defines our success. In this subchapter, we will explore effective strategies to cope with setbacks and failure, harnessing the power of motivation to bounce back stronger than ever.

One of the most important things to remember when facing setbacks is to embrace a growth mindset. Instead of viewing failure as a reflection of our worth or abilities, we should see it as an opportunity for growth and learning. Every setback presents a chance to reassess our approach, make necessary adjustments, and move forward with renewed vigor. By reframing setbacks as stepping stones to success, we can maintain our motivation and resilience.

Another crucial aspect of coping with setbacks is practicing self-compassion. It is natural to feel disappointed and discouraged when things don't go as planned. However, instead of wallowing in self-pity, we should be kind to ourselves and acknowledge that setbacks are a normal part of the journey towards success. By treating ourselves with compassion, we can regain our motivation and maintain a positive outlook despite the challenges we encounter.

Seeking support from others is also essential in coping with setbacks. Surrounding ourselves with a strong support network of friends, family, or mentors can provide valuable guidance, encouragement, and perspective. Sharing our experiences and discussing our setbacks with trusted individuals can help us gain insights and develop effective strategies to overcome obstacles. Additionally, connecting with like-minded individuals who have experienced similar setbacks can provide a sense of camaraderie and reassurance that we are not alone in our journey.

Lastly, it is important to maintain a long-term perspective when faced with setbacks. Success is rarely achieved overnight, and setbacks are often temporary roadblocks on the path to achieving our goals. By keeping our eyes on the bigger picture and reminding ourselves of our ultimate aspirations, we can stay motivated and resilient in the face of failure.

In conclusion, setbacks and failure are inevitable, but how we cope with them determines our ultimate success. By embracing a growth mindset, practicing self-compassion, seeking support, and maintaining a long-term perspective, we can harness the power of motivation to overcome setbacks and achieve our goals. Remember, setbacks are not the end of the road but rather opportunities for growth and improvement.

Chapter 8: Harnessing the Power of Motivation for Success

Applying Motivation to Personal and Professional Growth

Motivation is a powerful driving force that can propel individuals towards personal and professional growth. Whether you are a student, an employee, an entrepreneur, or anyone seeking success in life, understanding and harnessing the power of motivation can make a significant difference in achieving your goals.

Personal   Growth:
Motivation plays a crucial role in personal growth by igniting the desire to improve oneself and reach new heights. It acts as a catalyst for change, pushing individuals to step out of their comfort zones and embrace new challenges. By setting clear goals and creating a roadmap towards their achievement, motivated individuals can enhance their skills, knowledge, and overall personal development. Motivation helps in building resilience and perseverance, enabling individuals to overcome setbacks and obstacles along the way. It encourages self-reflection, self-discipline, and a positive mindset, leading to increased self-confidence and a sense of fulfillment.

Professional   Growth:
In the professional realm, motivation is the key to unlocking one's true potential. It inspires individuals to strive for excellence, take initiative, and continuously improve their performance. Motivated professionals are driven to acquire new skills, seek out opportunities for growth, and take on challenging projects. They exhibit a strong work ethic, dedication, and a passion for what they do. Motivation also fosters a sense of responsibility and accountability, as individuals take ownership

of their work and strive to exceed expectations. Additionally, motivated professionals are more likely to be proactive, show leadership qualities, and build strong relationships with colleagues and superiors.

The Power of Motivation: Understanding the power of motivation is essential for achieving success. It acts as a fuel that keeps individuals focused, determined, and committed to their goals. Motivation provides the energy and enthusiasm needed to overcome obstacles, persist through failures, and maintain a positive attitude. It helps individuals prioritize their tasks, manage their time effectively, and make the most of their abilities. Moreover, motivation breeds passion and a sense of purpose, allowing individuals to find joy and fulfillment in their personal and professional endeavors.

In conclusion, motivation has the power to transform lives and fuel success. By applying motivation to personal and professional growth, individuals can unleash their true potential, achieve their goals, and create a fulfilling life. Whether you are a student, an employee, or anyone seeking to make a positive change, harnessing the power of motivation is the key to unlocking a world of possibilities. So, embrace motivation, set ambitious goals, and let it guide you towards a future filled with growth, success, and happiness.

Achieving Long-Term Success Through Sustained Motivation

Success is not a one-time achievement; it is a continuous journey that requires sustained motivation. In this subchapter, we will explore how to fuel your success by harnessing the power of motivation.

Motivation is the driving force behind every successful individual. It is the spark that ignites passion, determination, and perseverance. However, motivation is not a one-size-fits-all concept. Different individuals are motivated by different factors. Understanding what motivates you personally is crucial in maintaining long-term success.

One key aspect of sustained motivation is setting meaningful goals. Without clear objectives, it is challenging to stay motivated. Set both short-term and long-term goals that align with your values and aspirations. These goals will serve as a roadmap, guiding your actions and keeping you focused.

Another important factor in sustaining motivation is maintaining a positive mindset. Negativity and self-doubt can hinder your progress. Surround yourself with positive influences, practice self-affirmations, and celebrate even the smallest victories. Remember that setbacks are part of the journey, and with a positive mindset, you can turn them into opportunities for growth.

Accountability is another powerful motivator. Share your goals with a trusted friend or mentor who can hold you accountable. Regular check-ins and feedback will help you stay on track and motivated. Additionally, consider joining a like-minded community or group where you can share experiences, challenges, and successes. The support and encouragement of others can be a great source of motivation.

To maintain sustained motivation, it is crucial to take care of your physical and mental well-being. Exercise regularly, eat a balanced diet, and get enough sleep. Physical health impacts mental well-being, and both are necessary for maintaining motivation. Engage in activities that bring you joy and help you relax, such as hobbies or spending time with loved ones. Taking care of yourself will ensure you have the energy and mental clarity to pursue your goals.

Finally, it is important to regularly reassess your motivations and goals. As you grow and evolve, your motivations may change. Reflect on your progress and adjust your goals accordingly. This self-reflection will help you maintain long-term success and ensure your motivations remain aligned with your true passions.

In conclusion, sustained motivation is the key to achieving long-term success. By understanding what motivates you, setting meaningful goals, maintaining a positive mindset, being accountable, taking care of your well-being, and regularly reassessing your motivations, you can fuel your success and create a fulfilling and prosperous life. Remember, motivation is not a finite resource; it is a powerful tool that, when harnessed effectively, can propel you towards greatness.

Inspiring Others to Fuel Their Own Success

In the journey towards success, one of the most fulfilling and impactful experiences is inspiring others to fuel their own success. When we share our motivation and drive with those around us, we create a ripple effect of positive change that can transform lives and communities. This subchapter delves into the power of motivation and how we can inspire others to unlock their full potential.

Motivation is a force that propels us forward, pushing us to overcome obstacles, set ambitious goals, and achieve greatness. It is the driving factor behind every successful individual, and its power is undeniable. By understanding the power of motivation, we gain the ability to ignite a spark within others and help them unlock their own potential.

To inspire others, we must first lead by example. By embodying our own motivation and pursuing our goals with unwavering determination, we show others what is possible. Our actions become a testament to the power of motivation, and others will be inspired by our resilience and success.

Another way to inspire others is by sharing our stories. Each of us has faced challenges and setbacks along our journey. By openly sharing our struggles and triumphs, we demonstrate that success is not a linear path but a series of ups and downs. Through our vulnerability, we can connect with others on a deeper level and inspire them to persevere in the face of adversity.

Additionally, we can provide guidance and support to those seeking motivation. By offering mentorship, coaching, or simply lending a listening ear, we become a source of encouragement for others. Through our guidance, we can help individuals identify their passions, set meaningful goals, and develop strategies to overcome obstacles. By empowering others with the tools and mindset needed for success, we can create a ripple effect that extends far beyond our immediate sphere of influence.

Ultimately, inspiring others to fuel their own success is a testament to the transformative power of motivation. By leading by example, sharing our stories, and providing guidance, we can ignite a fire within others that fuels their journey towards success. As we inspire others, we contribute to the growth and development of our communities, creating a world where everyone can reach their fullest potential. Let us embrace the power of motivation and empower others to unlock their own success.

Chapter 9: Strategies for Maintaining Motivation

Setting Realistic Goals and Milestones

In the journey towards success, setting realistic goals and milestones plays a crucial role in harnessing the power of motivation. Whether you are an aspiring entrepreneur, a student, or a professional looking to achieve personal growth, understanding how to set achievable targets is vital for sustained progress and fulfillment.

Firstly, it is essential to recognize that setting realistic goals is not synonymous with limiting one's ambitions. On the contrary, it involves taking a pragmatic approach to ensure that the objectives you set are within your reach, yet challenging enough to keep you engaged and motivated. By acknowledging your strengths, weaknesses, and available resources, you can set goals that are both attainable and inspiring.

To begin with, it is crucial to define your long-term objectives. What is it that you truly desire to achieve in your personal or professional life? These overarching goals will serve as the guiding light in your journey. However, instead of solely focusing on the end result, break down these long-term goals into smaller, manageable milestones. These milestones act as stepping stones, allowing you to measure progress and stay motivated throughout the process.

Furthermore, it is important to set specific, measurable, achievable, relevant, and time-bound (SMART) goals. When your goals are specific and measurable, you can track your progress and evaluate whether you are on the right path. Additionally, ensure that your goals are relevant to your aspirations and align with your values and priorities. This will provide a sense of purpose and make your efforts more meaningful.

Setting a timeline for your goals is equally important. By assigning deadlines to your milestones, you create a sense of urgency and prevent procrastination. However, be mindful of setting realistic timeframes that consider potential obstacles or unexpected circumstances. This will prevent disappointment and frustration if you encounter delays or setbacks along the way.

Regularly reviewing and adjusting your goals is also crucial for maintaining motivation and progress. As you move forward, reassess your goals and milestones periodically to ensure they remain relevant and achievable. Adjusting your targets based on your evolving circumstances and experiences will help you stay focused and adapt to any unforeseen challenges.

In conclusion, setting realistic goals and milestones is a fundamental aspect of harnessing the power of motivation. By breaking down your long-term objectives into smaller, manageable milestones and aligning them with the SMART criteria, you can ensure that your goals are both attainable and inspiring. Regularly reviewing and adjusting your goals will keep you motivated and adaptable in the face of obstacles. Remember, success is not just about the end result; it is the journey towards achieving your aspirations that truly fuels your motivation.

Celebrating Small Wins and Progress

In the journey towards success, it is crucial to acknowledge and celebrate the small wins and progress we make along the way. These small victories are like stepping stones that lead us to our ultimate goals. They not only provide motivation but also boost our confidence and drive to keep pushing forward.

When we set big, audacious goals, it is easy to become overwhelmed and discouraged by the enormity of the task at hand. However, by recognizing the small wins, we break down the larger goal into manageable chunks, making the process feel less daunting. Each small achievement serves as a reminder that we are making progress, no matter how small it may seem.

Celebrating these small wins is essential because it reinforces the belief that we are capable of achieving our goals. It instills a sense of accomplishment and satisfaction, which in turn fuels us to continue working towards our dreams. Moreover, celebrating small wins helps to cultivate a positive mindset, enabling us to stay motivated even during challenging times.

One powerful way to celebrate small wins is by practicing gratitude. Take a moment to express appreciation for the progress you have made and acknowledge the effort you have put in. This can be as simple as journaling about your achievements or sharing them with a supportive friend or mentor. By expressing gratitude, you create a positive feedback loop that encourages further progress and motivates you to keep going.

Another effective way to celebrate small wins is by rewarding yourself. Treat yourself to something you enjoy after reaching a milestone or completing a task. This could be indulging in a favorite meal, taking a day off to relax, or buying something you have been wanting. By rewarding yourself, you reinforce the positive behavior and create anticipation and excitement for future achievements.

In conclusion, celebrating small wins and progress is vital in keeping the motivation alive on our journey to success. By acknowledging these milestones, we build confidence, reinforce positive behaviors, and cultivate a mindset of gratitude. So, let us take a moment to recognize and celebrate each small win, knowing that they are all stepping stones that will lead us to our ultimate success.

Continuously Learning and Adapting

In the journey towards success, one of the most vital attributes to possess is the ability to continuously learn and adapt. The power of motivation lies in its ability to fuel this constant growth and evolution. Whether you are an aspiring entrepreneur, a student, or a professional in any field, embracing a mindset of continuous learning and adaptation is crucial in achieving your goals and reaching new heights.

Learning is not limited to the formal education system; it extends far beyond that. It is a lifelong process that should be embraced with enthusiasm and an open mind. By consistently seeking knowledge and expanding your skill set, you equip yourself with the tools necessary to excel in your chosen field. This can be achieved through various means such as reading books, attending workshops and seminars, enrolling in online courses, or even engaging in meaningful conversations with experts in your industry.

Adaptation, on the other hand, is the ability to adjust and thrive in the face of change. The world is constantly evolving, and it is those who can adapt quickly and effectively that will succeed. Adapting requires a willingness to step out of your comfort zone, embrace new technologies, and be open to different perspectives. By doing so, you become more resilient, versatile, and better equipped to navigate the challenges that come your way.

Continuous learning and adaptation go hand in hand. When you commit to constantly learning, you become more adaptable. And when you adapt, you create opportunities for further growth and development. The power of motivation lies in its ability to drive you towards this continuous cycle of learning and adaptation.

To foster a mindset of continuous learning and adaptation, it is important to cultivate certain habits. Firstly, be curious. Ask questions, seek answers, and have an insatiable thirst for knowledge. Secondly, be proactive. Take the initiative to seek out learning opportunities and stay ahead of the curve. Thirdly, embrace failures and setbacks as learning experiences. Instead of viewing them as roadblocks, see them as stepping stones towards improvement and growth.

Ultimately, the power of motivation lies in its ability to fuel your desire to continuously learn and adapt. By embracing this mindset, you position yourself for success in any field. So, let motivation be the driving force behind your journey of growth and development, propelling you towards new levels of success and fulfillment.

Chapter 10: Case Studies of Motivational Success Stories

Exemplary Individuals Who Achieved Greatness Through Motivation

In the vast realm of human history, there have been individuals who have achieved greatness through the sheer power of motivation. These exceptional individuals serve as shining examples of what can be accomplished when one is fueled by a burning desire to succeed. Their stories not only inspire and uplift, but they also provide valuable insights into the power of motivation and its potential to transform lives.

One such exemplary individual is Helen Keller, who overcame the dual challenges of blindness and deafness to become a renowned author, lecturer, and political activist. Despite her physical limitations, Keller's unwavering determination and indomitable spirit led her to conquer seemingly insurmountable obstacles. Her story teaches us that no matter how challenging our circumstances may be, with the right mindset and relentless motivation, we can achieve greatness.

Another individual who exemplifies the power of motivation is Mahatma Gandhi. Known as the father of India, Gandhi played a pivotal role in India's struggle for independence from British rule. His philosophy of non-violence and his unwavering commitment to truth and justice continue to inspire people around the world. Gandhi's motivation stemmed from his deep love for humanity and his unyielding belief in the power of peaceful resistance. His story teaches us that when we are motivated by a higher purpose and a genuine desire to make a positive impact, we can move mountains and change the world.

There is also the remarkable story of Oprah Winfrey, who rose from a troubled childhood to become one of the most influential media moguls of our time. Through sheer determination, perseverance, and a relentless drive to succeed, Winfrey transformed her life and used her platform to empower and inspire millions of individuals worldwide. Her story serves as a testament to the fact that motivation, when channeled effectively, can propel us towards unimaginable heights of success.

These exemplary individuals not only achieved greatness themselves but also ignited a spark within others, encouraging them to harness the power of motivation in their own lives. Their stories teach us that motivation is not just a fleeting emotion but a force that, when properly channeled, can drive us towards achieving our dreams and making a positive impact on the world around us.

In conclusion, the power of motivation is a force that has the potential to transform lives and lead individuals to achieve greatness. Through the inspiring stories of individuals like Helen Keller, Mahatma Gandhi, and Oprah Winfrey, we learn that motivation, when combined with determination, resilience, and a higher purpose, can overcome any obstacle and fuel our journey towards success. These exemplary individuals serve as beacons of hope and inspiration for anyone seeking to tap into their own inner motivation and unleash their full potential.

Analyzing the Strategies and Mindsets of Successful People

Success is a goal that many of us aspire to achieve, but what separates those who actually achieve it from those who don't? The answer lies in the strategies and mindsets of successful people. In this subchapter, we will dive deep into the strategies and mindsets that fuel the success of these individuals, examining the power of motivation and how it plays a crucial role in their achievements.

One of the key strategies employed by successful people is goal setting. They have a clear vision of what they want to achieve and set specific, measurable, achievable, relevant, and time-bound (SMART) goals to guide their actions. Moreover, they break down their goals into smaller, manageable tasks, allowing them to stay focused and motivated throughout the journey.

Another crucial aspect of success is self-belief. Successful individuals have an unwavering belief in their abilities and potential. They understand that setbacks and failures are part of the process, but they do not let them define their worth or deter them from their goals. This mindset allows them to bounce back stronger and learn from their experiences.

Successful people also understand the power of perseverance. They embrace challenges and view them as opportunities for growth. Instead of giving up at the first sign of adversity, they persist and push through, knowing that the road to success is rarely smooth. This resilience separates them from the rest, as they are willing to put in the extra effort and go the extra mile to achieve their dreams.

Additionally, successful individuals surround themselves with a strong support network. They understand the importance of having mentors, role models, and like-minded individuals who can provide guidance, support, and motivation. This network acts as a source of inspiration and accountability, helping them stay focused on their goals.

Lastly, successful people continuously seek opportunities for self-improvement. They are lifelong learners, always hungry for knowledge and growth. They invest in personal development through reading books, attending seminars, and seeking out new experiences. This commitment to learning enables them to stay ahead of the game and adapt to the ever-changing world.

In conclusion, analyzing the strategies and mindsets of successful people is an enlightening exercise that sheds light on the power of motivation. By understanding and implementing these strategies in our own lives, we too can fuel our success. It all starts with setting clear goals, believing in ourselves, persevering through challenges, building a strong support network, and committing to lifelong learning. With motivation as our driving force, we can overcome obstacles and achieve the success we desire.

Lessons Learned from Motivational Role Models

In our journey towards success, motivation plays a crucial role. It is the driving force that pushes us to overcome obstacles, achieve our goals, and reach our full potential. While motivation can come from within, it is often helpful to look to role models who have already achieved great success for inspiration and guidance. These individuals can provide us with valuable lessons that can fuel our own motivation and propel us towards our own success.

One of the key lessons we can learn from motivational role models is the importance of setting clear goals. Successful individuals understand that without a clear vision of what they want to achieve, their motivation can wane. By setting specific, measurable, achievable, relevant, and time-bound (SMART) goals, we can align our efforts and stay focused on our path to success.

Another lesson we can learn is the power of perseverance. Motivational role models have often faced numerous setbacks and failures on their journey to success. However, they did not let these challenges deter them. Instead, they used them as stepping stones towards their goals. They understood that failure is not the end but rather a valuable opportunity to learn, grow, and adapt. By embracing failure and persisting through adversity, we can develop resilience and keep our motivation alive even in the face of setbacks.

Motivational role models also teach us the importance of self-belief. They demonstrate that having confidence in our abilities and believing in ourselves is essential for success. By cultivating a positive mindset and eliminating self-doubt, we can tap into our full potential and overcome any obstacles that come our way.

Furthermore, these role models remind us of the significance of taking action. It is not enough to dream or have good intentions; we must actively pursue our goals. Motivation without action is merely wishful thinking. By taking consistent and focused action towards our goals, we can turn our dreams into reality.

Lastly, motivational role models teach us the power of gratitude and giving back. They understand that success is not only about personal achievement but also about making a positive impact on others and the world. By expressing gratitude for what we have and helping others along the way, we can find fulfillment and sustain our motivation for the long haul.

In conclusion, the lessons learned from motivational role models can be invaluable in fueling our own success. By setting clear goals, persevering through challenges, believing in ourselves, taking action, and practicing gratitude, we can harness the power of motivation to achieve our dreams. Let us look to these role models as inspiration and guidance as we embark on our own journey towards success.

Conclusion: Fueling Your Success: Embracing the Power of Motivation

Conclusion: Fueling Your Success: Embracing the Power of Motivation

In this journey of discovering the power of motivation, we have explored the depths of its impact on our lives. We have learned that motivation is not just a fleeting feeling or an external force, but a driving force within us that can shape our destiny. It is the fuel that propels us forward, igniting our passion and determination to achieve greatness.

Motivation is not limited to a select few; it is accessible to anyone who is willing to embrace its power. It does not discriminate based on age, gender, background, or circumstances. Whether you are a student striving for academic success, an entrepreneur seeking to build a thriving business, or an individual looking to make a positive change in your life, motivation can be your guiding light.

Through this book, we have explored various strategies and techniques to harness the power of motivation. We have delved into the importance of setting clear goals, visualizing success, and developing a growth mindset. We have discussed the significance of surrounding ourselves with positive influences, practicing self-care, and overcoming obstacles with resilience.

But the true power of motivation lies in our ability to take action. It is not enough to simply understand its significance; we must actively embrace it in our daily lives. We must cultivate a burning desire within us, a relentless pursuit of our dreams and aspirations.

Fueling your success requires discipline, dedication, and perseverance. It demands that you push beyond your comfort zone and embrace challenges as opportunities for growth. It asks you to believe in yourself, even when the odds seem insurmountable.

Remember, motivation is not a one-time occurrence; it is a continuous process. It requires consistent effort and a commitment to personal growth. It is about finding the inner drive to keep going, even when faced with setbacks or failures.

As you embark on your journey towards success, remember that motivation is your greatest ally. It is the force that will propel you forward, even in the face of adversity. Embrace its power, nurture it, and let it guide you towards the fulfillment of your dreams.

Fueling your success begins with a single step – the decision to believe in yourself and the power of motivation. So, take that step today and set yourself on a path towards greatness. You have the power within you to achieve anything you set your mind to. Embrace it, harness it, and let it fuel your success.

www.ingramcontent.com/pod-product-compliance
Lightning Source LLC
LaVergne TN
LVHW020939200726
843506LV00011B/2055